The Perfect Pizza

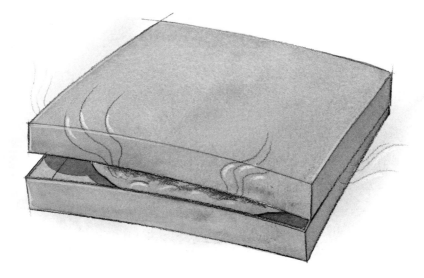

Charlie Walker
Illustrated by Julian Bruere

"What comes in a box like this?"
asked Mrs. Lee.

"Pizza!" we said.

"What pizza toppings do you like best?"
asked Mrs. Lee.

"I like pepperoni!" said Justin.

"How many of you like pepperoni?"
asked Mrs. Lee.

Pepperoni

"I like mushrooms!" said Mary.

"How many of you like mushrooms?" asked Mrs. Lee.

Pepperoni 11/1

Mushrooms

"I like peppers!" said Juan.

"How many of you like peppers?" asked Mrs. Lee.

Pepperoni ||/|
Mushrooms ||
Peppers

"Most of us like pepperoni best,"
said Alex.

"We can show that in a graph,"
said Mrs. Lee.

Pepperoni IIII

Mushrooms II

Peppers II

10

We helped make a graph.

"Now it's easy to see
that most of us like pepperoni best,"
said Alex.

"Let's make a picture of a pizza
to match the graph," said Mrs. Lee.

We made a pizza out of paper.

"It's a picture of our perfect pizza!"
said Emiko.

The next day our pizza picture was on the wall.

"That picture makes me hungry," said Juan.

"I have a surprise for everyone," said Mrs. Lee.

"It's the real perfect pizza!"
we cheered.
"Let's eat!"